The I Slow Cooker Cookbook

60 Best Fix&Forget Crock Pot Recipes for your Home Collection

Sara Parker

Copyright by Sara Parker - All rights reserved.

No part of this publication may be reproduced or transmitted in any form or by any means, mechanical or electronic, including photocopying and recording, or by any information storage and retrieval system, without permission, in written, from the author.

All attempts have been made to verify information provided in this publication. Neither the author nor the publisher assumes any responsibility for errors or omissions of the subject matter herein. This publication is not intended for use as a source of legal or accounting advice. The Publisher wants to stress that the information contained herein may be subject to varying state and/or local laws or regulations. All users are advised to retain competent counsel to determine what state and/or local laws or regulations may apply to the user's particular business.

The purchaser or reader of this publication assumes responsibility for the use of these materials and information. Adherence to all applicable laws and regulations, federal, state, and local, governing professional licensing, business practices, advertising, and all other aspects of doing business in the United States or any other jurisdiction is the sole responsibility of the purchaser or reader.

The author and Publisher assume no responsibility or liability whatsoever on the behalf of any purchaser or reader of these materials for injury due to use of any of the methods contained herein. Any perceived slights of specific people or organizations are unintentional.

Table of Contents

TABLE OF CONTENTS 4

INTRODUCTION 7

SLOW FOOD – GOOD FOOD 8

    6 BENEFITS OF SLOW COOKING 8

COOKING MEASUREMENT CONVERSION CHART 10

OPTIMIZE YOUR METABOLISM 11

WEIGHT LOSS DIET TIPS THAT REALLY WORK 12

BREAKFAST RECIPES 13

    HEALTHY OVERNIGHT STEEL CUT OATS 13
    APPETIZING CHICKEN CAESAR SANDWICH 14
    DELICIOUS OATMEAL WITH APPLES 15
    AMAZING FRENCH TOAST CASSEROLE 16
    STEEL-CUT OATS WITH HONEY 17
    PUMPKIN SPICE CLEAN EATING POT OATMEAL 18
    HOMEMADE GREEK YOGURT 19
    ITALIAN SPICY OMELETTE 20
    MORNING OATMEAL WITH DRIED FRUITS 21
    DELICIOUS BREAKFAST HASH BROWN 22

APPETIZERS 23

    DELICIOUS PARMESAN-CRUSTED CHICKEN 23
    CROCK POT CHEESE FONDUE 24
    SIMPLE BBQ RIBS 25
    BROCCOLI & BACON CHEESY APPETIZER 26
    CROCK POT CHIPOTLE CHILI 27

BUTTERNUT SQUASH RISOTTO WITH GOAT CHEESE 28
GREEN BEAN CASSEROLE 29

MAIN DISHES 30

POTATOES WITH BACON & BEANS 30
PORK ROAST IN MUSTARD SAUCE 31
SWEET POTATO STEW WITH CHICKEN 32
OUTSTANDING SWEET PORK 33
CREAMY POTATOES WITH BRATWURST SAUSAGE 34
SWEET CHICKEN BREAST WITH HONEY 35
SLOW COOKER CHICKEN ADOBO 36
FAMOUS SANTA FE CHICKEN 37
AMAZING TENDER CHICKEN WITH MUSHROOMS 39
SPICY PORK CHILI 41
ADORABLE CROCKPOT ITALIAN CHICKEN 42
JERKY CHICKEN 43
POTATO STEW WITH VEGETABLES AND SPICES 44
BUFFALO CHICKEN PASTA 46
PORK CHOPS WITH TOMATOES 47
HERBS & WINE VEAL 48
PORK CHOPS BARBECUE WITH APPLES AND ONIONS 49
BLACK BEANS AND BEEF STEW 50
ASIAN PORK CHOPS 51
CLEAN EATING CROCK POT CHUCK ROAST 52
SLOW COOKER BEEF BRISKET 53
SMOKED UP BABY POTATOES WITH BEEF 54
BEER CHILI BEANS WITH BRATWURST SAUSAGE 56
TENDER BEEF STROGANOFF 57
SWEET POTATOES WITH COCONUT AND PECANS 58
EASY BEEF STEAK 59

SIDE DISHES 60

JAMAICAN CURRY CHICKEN 60

- DELICIOUS CHICKEN WITH MUSHROOMS 61
- BEEF AND BROCCOLI PENNE 62
- SALSA CHICKEN IN SOUR CREAM 63
- CREOLE CHICKEN STEW 64
- CREAMY CHICKEN WITH NOODLES 66
- CHICKEN PAPRIKASH NOODLES 67

SOUP RECIPES 68
- EASY POTATO SOUP 68
- SPICY BEAN SOUP WITH TURKEY 70
- KALE SOUP WITH ITALIAN SAUSAGE 71
- CHICKEN TOMATO SOUP 72
- DELICIOUS VEGETABLE SOUP WITH BEEF CHUNKS 73
- MEATY BARLEY LENTIL SOUP 74

SNACKS AND DESSERTS 75
- CARAMELIZED ONIONS 75
- SLOW COOKER APPLES 76
- CROCK POT STEWED PLUMS 77
- PEANUTS WITH CHOCOLATE 78

CONCLUSION 79

Introduction

I cook because I love to cook. This is my passion and I cannot live without cooking. All this goes from childhood when I lived with my parents. I remember my mother always cooked various delicious dishes using many devices. Slow Cooker was one of these kitchen appliances that helped mom create superb meals for the whole family.

A lot of time has passed since that moment. Now I'm living separately for a long time, but my love for cooking only grew from year to year. Slow Cooker became one of my favorite kitchen appliances. The key advantage of this device is that I can cook healthy and delicious dishes without spending time on it. I just need to load needed ingredients according to the chosen recipe, choose the necessary program and continue to do your own household chores. Moreover, I can even turn on my Slow Cooker in the morning and go to work. And in the evening, me and my family will receive a delicious and hot dinner from my favorite Slow Cooker!

In this cookbook you will find a great variety of recipes for all occasions. You will get recipes for healthy and hearty breakfasts, excellent snacks for large companies, meat and poultry dishes, vegetable recipes and even desserts. All that you lacked in your other cookbooks you can find in HERE!

Slow Food – Good Food

Preparing your favorite meals with the help of Slow Cocker is becoming more popular. Of course, each of us has his own favorite devices and favorite recipes, but Slow Cooker also has many advantages that will allow you to look at this kitchen device in a different way.

Slow Cooker helps to prepare delicious dishes for hundreds years and with it's help you can cook almost anything: breakfasts, side dishes, courses, meat and vegetable dishes, desserts.

6 Benefits of Slow Cooking

There are numerous reasons to love Slow Cooker. Here are just a few of the main advantages, however, the more you'll use this device in the kitchen, this list will increase.

Time-saver device
From now you are not a slave in your kitchen. All time you need is only for preparation, no more than 10-15 minutes. Your slow cooker will do all the job while you are doing anything else.

One-pot dishes
You can cook your favorite dishes without a lot of dishes for washing. Slow cooker is the perfect device for one-pot dishes. Just load prepared ingredients, turn on the device and that's all!

Delicious & healthy dishes
Since preparing in the slow cooker is mainly using fresh ingredients, a low cooking temperature leaves a numerous useful components. Vegetables and meat cooked in the slow cooker give off a lot of juices, soak them up, mix, giving a fuller flavor.

Easy cleaning
Thanks to the fact that only one device is used, washing it is much easier and faster than a huge number of pans, pots and other appliances.

Usage all year round
Slow cooker is the ideal device for cooking vegetables. Therefore it is perfect for cooking dishes from summer vegetables such as zucchini, broccoli, tomatoes and peppers, and from winter ones - pumpkin, carrots, potatoes and so on.

Eco-friendly
Due to the fact that cooking temperature is significantly reduced, you use less energy. Thus, cooking in the slow cooker is an eco friendly and allows you to use two times less energy.

Cooking Measurement Conversion Chart

Liquid Measures

1 gal = 4 qt = 8 pt = 16 cups = 128 fl oz
½ gal = 2 qt = 4 pt = 8 cups = 64 fl oz
¼ gal = 1 qt = 2 pt = 4 cups = 32 fl oz
½ qt = 1 pt = 2 cups = 16 fl oz
¼ qt = ½ pt = 1 cup = 8 fl oz

Dry Measures

1 cup = 16 Tbsp = 48 tsp = 250ml
¾ cup = 12 Tbsp = 36 tsp = 175ml
⅔ cup = 10 ⅔ Tbsp = 32 tsp = 150ml
½ cup = 8 Tbsp = 24 tsp = 125ml
⅓ cup = 5 ⅓ Tbsp = 16 tsp = 75ml
¼ cup = 4 Tbsp = 12 tsp = 50ml
⅛ cup = 2 Tbsp = 6 tsp = 30ml
1 Tbsp = 3 tsp = 15ml

Dash or Pinch or Speck = less than ⅛ tsp

Quickies

1 fl oz = 30 ml
1 oz = 28.35 g
1 lb = 16 oz (454 g)
1 kg = 2.2 lb
1 quart = 2 pints

U.S.	Canadian
¼ tsp	1.25 mL
½ tsp	2.5 mL
1 tsp	5 mL
1 Tbl	15 mL
¼ cup	50 mL
⅓ cup	75 mL
½ cup	125 mL
⅔ cup	150 mL
¾ cup	175 mL
1 cup	250 mL
1 quart	1 liter

Recipe Abbreviations

Cup = c or C
Fluid = fl
Gallon = gal
Ounce = oz
Package = pkg
Pint = pt
Pound = lb or #
Quart = qt
Square = sq
Tablespoon = T or Tbl or TBSP or TBS
Teaspoon = t or tsp

*Some measurements were rounded

Fahrenheit (°F) to Celcius (°C)

$°C = (°F - 32) \times 5/9$

°F	°C
32°F	0°C
40°F	4°C
140°F	60°C
150°F	65°C
160°F	70°C
225°F	107°C
250°F	121°C
275°F	135°C
300°F	150°C
325°F	165°C
350°F	177°C
375°F	190°C
400°F	205°C
425°F	220°C
450°F	230°C
475°F	245°C
500°F	260°C

OVEN TEMPERATURES

WARMING: 200°F
VERY SLOW: 250°F - 275°F
SLOW: 300°F - 325°F
MODERATE: 350°F - 375°F
HOT: 400°F - 425°F
VERY HOT: 450°F - 475°F

Optimize your Metabolism

Optimizing metabolism is a main key to weight loss. It means that you will burn more calories even when you're rest, even without physical workout. Here's useful chart with 12 main foods which will boost your metabolism. Just include as many of these products as you can in your daily diet and get a great opportunity to control your weight and create a perfect body!

Weight Loss Diet Tips that Really Work

Please also check main weight loss tips which can help you control body weight.

Breakfast Recipes

Healthy Overnight Steel Cut Oats

Prep time: 12 minutes, cook time: 6-7 hours, ingredients: 5-6

Ingredients

- 1 - ½ cups frozen blueberries (or another berries on your preference)
- 2 cups water
- 1 cup skimmed milk
- 1 large banana, mashed
- 1 cup steel cut oats
- 1 teaspoon ground cinnamon
- 1 tablespoon sugar (optional)
- Honey for serving

Directions

1. Pour in water and milk in a slow cooker.
2. Add mashed banana, frozen berries, and steel cut oats. Season with ground cinnamon.
3. Cover and cook on high for about 1 hour. When timer beeps, switch to "warm" and cook overnight (for about 6-8 hours).
4. Serve with honey or sugar.

Appetizing Chicken Caesar Sandwich

Prep time: 10 minutes, cook time: 4-5 hours, servings: 4-6

Ingredients

- 2 pounds chicken breasts, boneless and skinless
- ½ cup Caesar dressing
- ½ cup parmesan cheese, shredded
- ¼ cup fresh parsley, chopped
- ½ teaspoon ground pepper
- 2 cups romaine lettuce, shredded
- 4-6 regular size hamburger buns

Preparation

1. Put chicken breasts into the slow cooker, pour 1-2 cups of water over, cover and cook on low for 4-5 hours.
2. Remove cooked chicken from the Crockpot, drain the water from the slow cooker.
3. Shred the chicken using two forks and discarding any fat.
4. Place shredded chicken back to the slow cooker and pour dressing, parmesan cheese, parsley and pepper over.
5. Stir evenly.
6. Cover and cook for another 30 minutes or until ready.
7. Spoon the mixture into each slider bun.
8. Top with extra parmesan cheese and lettuce and serve.

Delicious Oatmeal with Apples

Prep time: 10 minutes, cook time: 4-5 hours, servings: 4-5

Ingredients

- 1 tablespoon butter
- 1 cup dried oatmeal
- 1 large apple, peeled and sliced
- 2 cups milk
- 1-2 tablespoons honey
- A pinch of salt
- Brown sugar and nuts for garnish

Directions

1. Add oatmeal, sliced apple, milk, honey, and salt in a large bowl. Stir to combine.
2. Grease a slow cooker with butter and pour in prepared mixture.
3. Cover and cook on high for 4 hours.
4. Serve into individual plates and garnish with brown sugar and nuts.

Amazing French Toast Casserole
Prep time: 5 minutes, cook time: 6 hours, servings: 8

Ingredients

- ½ pound bread, cut into 1-inch cubes
- 6 large eggs
- 1 cup whole milk
- 1 teaspoon almond extract
- 1 cup of half and half
- 1 teaspoon of lemon zest, grated
- ¼ teaspoon ground cloves
- ¼ teaspoon ground cinnamon
- ½ teaspoon vanilla extract
- 3 tablespoons sugar
- 1 cup almonds

Directions

1. Preheat the oven for 230 F and bake bread cubes for 30 minutes, until become crunchy.
2. Place bread cubes on the bottom of slow cooker pot.
3. In the medium bowl combine lemon zest, eggs, almond extract, half and half, cinnamon, ground cloves. Mix well and pour the mixture in a slow cooker. Top with almonds and cook on low for 4-5 hours.
4. When ready serve with honey or maple syrup.

Steel-Cut Oats with Honey

Prep time: 2 minutes, cook time: 3-4 hours, servings: 6

Ingredients

- 1 cup steel-cut oatmeal
- 1 cup skimmed milk
- 2 cups water
- 4 tablespoons almond butter
- 5-6 tablespoons honey
- Salt, to taste

Directions

1. In a large bowl combine water, milk and steel-cut oatmeal. Season with salt and mix well.
2. Transfer the mixture to a slow cooker, close the lid and cook in high for 3-4 hours.
3. When ready, stir in almond butter, top with honey and serve.

Pumpkin Spice Clean Eating Pot Oatmeal

Prep time: 15 minutes, cook time: 4 hours, servings: 8

Ingredients

- 2 cups of steel cut oats
- 1 can (15 oz) pumpkin puree
- 1 tablespoon softened butter
- 4 cups water
- 1 cup milk
- ¼ cup maple syrup
- 2 tablespoons brown sugar
- 1 tablespoon vanilla
- ¼ teaspoon cinnamon

Directions

1. Grease the slow cooker pot with butter.
2. In the large bowl combine all ingredients, including steel cut oats, water, milk, maple syrup, sugar, vanilla and cinnamon. Whisk evenly.
3. Pour the mixture to a slow cooker, close the lid and cook on low for 4 hours.
4. Serve and enjoy.

Homemade Greek Yogurt
Prep time: 5 minutes, cook time: 7 hours, servings: 8

Ingredients

- 16 cups whole milk
- 1 cup plain yogurt (must have live cultures)

Directions

1. Add whole milk to your crock pot. Close the lid and cook on high for 2-3 hours.
2. Open the lid and using thermometer check the temperature. It need to be not more than 110 F. If milk is hot set aside to chill.
3. When temperature is OK, stir in plain yogurt, mix well and close the lid. Wrap crock pot with a warm kitchen towel and set aside for 8 hours.
4. Open the lid and ladle your Greek yogurt to a plate. You may use any topping you like: nuts, honey, cinnamon, brown sugar or anything else.

Italian Spicy Omelette

Prep time: 5 minutes, cook time: 2 hours, servings: 4

Ingredients

- 5-6 large eggs
- 1 cup cauliflower, cut into florets
- 1 cup skim milk
- ½ cup shredded Cheddar cheese
- ½ teaspoon dried basil
- ½ teaspoon dried oregano
- ½ teaspoon dried parsley
- ½ teaspoon dried dill
- ¼ teaspoon black pepper
- 2 small garlic cloves, minced
- A pinch of chili powder
- 1 tablespoon olive oil

Directions

1. Drizzle the crock pot with olive oil.
2. In the large mixing bowl combine milk, eggs and spices. Mix well. Then, stir in cauliflower florets, garlic cloves and 1/2 of cheese.
3. Pour the mixture to a slow cooker and close the lid. Cook for 2 hours on slow.
4. When ready, serve the omelette into plates and top with the remaining cheese.
5. Enjoy.

Morning Oatmeal with Dried Fruits
Prep time: 5 minutes, cook time: 8 hours, servings: 6

Ingredients

- 2 cups steel cut oats
- 1/2 cup dried berries
- ½ cup raisins
- ½ cup dried figs
- 1 tablespoon brown sugar
- 3 cups water
- 1 cup whole milk

Directions

1. Combine all ingredients in the slow cooker pot. Stir well and pour in water.
2. Close the lid and cook overnight on low for 8 hours.
3. Serve in the morning and get valuable and healthy breakfast!

Delicious Breakfast Hash Brown

Prep time: 10 minutes, cook time: 6 hours, servings: 10

Ingredients

- 1 pound cooked ham
- 1 bag frozen hash browns
- 4 garlic cloves, minced
- 1 medium sized onion, diced
- 1 cup shredded cheese
- 1 cup skim milk
- 10 large eggs
- ½ teaspoon salt
- ¼ teaspoon black pepper.
- ½ teaspoon dried thyme

Directions

1. Add ingredients to a slow cooker pot in the following order: 1/2 hash browns, 1/2 cooked ham, 1/2 onions 1/2 cheese. Then repeat layers in the same order.
2. In the mixing bowl combine milk, eggs, season with salt, pepper and thyme.
3. Pour the mixture into the crock pot and cook for 5-6 hours.
4. Serve and enjoy.

Appetizers

Delicious Parmesan-Crusted Chicken
Prep time: 10 minutes, cook time: 4-5 hours, servings: 5

Ingredients

- 2-3 chicken breasts, skinless
- ½ cup Italian seasoned breadcrumbs
- ¼ cup parmesan cheese, grated
- ¼ teaspoon ground black pepper
- ¼ teaspoon salt
- 1 tablespoon Olive oil
- 1 egg, beaten
- Sliced mozzarella cheese (optional)
- Favorite marinara sauce

Directions

1. Sprinkle 1 tablespoon of olive oil on the bottom of the slow cooker.
2. In a small bowl whisk the egg.
3. Mix Italian seasoned breadcrumbs, parmesan, ground pepper and salt in the middle bowl.
4. Dip the chicken into the egg and then into the breadcrumbs mixture. Evenly cover all sides of the chicken with egg and mixture.
5. Put the chicken breasts in the bottom of the crock pot.
6. Lay 3-4 slices of mozzarella cheese on top (optional).
7. Pour your favorite marinara sauce over chicken and cheese.

8. Close lid and prepare for low for 4-5 hours or until chicken becomes ready.

Crock Pot Cheese Fondue
Prep time: 10 minutes, cook time: 2 hours, servings: 3-4

Ingredients

- 1 tablespoon butter
- 1 small onion, chopped
- 1 garlic clove, minced
- 1 tablespoon all-purpose flour
- 5-6 tablespoons dry white wine
- 4 tablespoons skimmed milk
- ½ cup shredded Cheddar cheese
- ½ cup Gruyere cheese
- 2 oz Blue cheese

Directions

1. Add all ingredients to a large bowl. Pour in wine and milk and stir to combine.

Transfer the mixture to a slow cooker, cover and cook on low for 3-4 hours stirring couple time while cooking, until cheese melted

Simple BBQ Ribs

Prep time: 8 minutes, cook time: 6-8 hours, servings: 6

Ingredients

- 3 pounds pork loin ribs, boneless
- 3 tablespoon liquid smoke
- ½ cup brown sugar
- ½ cup sweet onion, diced
- 1 bottle (18 oz) favorite BBQ sauce

Directions

1. Cover slow cooker with cooking spray.
2. Rub pork ribs with liquid smoke. Place them into the slow cooker.
3. Sprinkle brown sugar over the top of the ribs.
4. Pour the bottle of your favorite BBQ sauce over the of the ribs.
5. Cover and cook on low for 6-8 hours until ribs become tender.

Broccoli & Bacon Cheesy Appetizer

Prep time: 15 minutes, cook time: 2 hours, servings: 10-12

Ingredients

- 1 can (10 oz) mushroom soup
- 14 slices cooked bacon
- 1 pound broccoli, cut into florets, and blanched
- 2 - ½ cups shredded Cheddar cheese
- 1/3 cup water
- 1 teaspoon mustard

Directions

1. Mix together canned soup, mustard, and water.
2. Place cooked bacon, blanched broccoli and shredded cheese into a slow cooker and pour the soup mixture over. Stir to combine well.
3. Cook on high for 1-2 hours and serve hot.

Crock Pot Chipotle Chili

Prep time: 15 minutes, cook time: 5 hours, servings: 5-6

Ingredients

- 1 - ½ pounds ground beef
- 1 large onion, diced
- 3 garlic cloves, minced
- 1 can (14 fl oz) black beans
- 1 can (14 fl oz) kidney beans
- 1 can (14 fl oz) pinto beans
- 2 cans (15 fl oz each) diced tomatoes
- 1 small can chipotle chilies in adobe sauce
- 2 teaspoons chili powder
- 1 teaspoon ground cumin
- ½ teaspoon salt
- ¼ teaspoon black pepper

Directions

1. Brown ground beef in a large skillet until no longer pink, for about 6-8 minutes. Transfer meat to a slow cooker basket.
2. Add onions and garlic on top.
3. Drain and rinse beans and also add them to a slow cooker. Add tomatoes and spices.
4. Cover and cook on high for 5 hours.
5. Sprinkle with freshly chopped parsley or dill (optional) and serve hot.

Butternut Squash Risotto with Goat Cheese

Prep time: 15 minutes, cook time: 6 hours, servings: 4

Ingredients

- 2 pounds butternut squash, peeled and cut into 1-inch pieces
- ¼ cup shallots, finely chopped
- ¼ cup dry white wine
- 2 cups chicken or vegetable stock
- 1 cup brown rice, uncooked
- ¾ cup goat cheese, crumbled
- 1 teaspoon olive oil
- ½ teaspoon salt
- ¼ teaspoon black pepper
- Fresh sage leaves (for garnish), chopped

Directions

1. Grease the crock pot with olive oil. Add chopped shallots and cook for 4 minutes using Sauté mode. Add butternut squash cut into 1-inch cubes, rice and pour in chicken or vegetable stock.
2. Close the lid and cook on low for 5-6 hours until rice cooked.
3. Stir in crumbled cheese.
4. Top with fresh sage leaves and serve.

Green Bean Casserole

Prep time: 13 minutes, cook time: 3 hours, servings: 4-6

Ingredients

- 2 can (15 oz) cut green beans, drained
- 1 can (10 oz) cream of mushroom soup, undiluted
- 1 package (8 oz) Cheddar cheese, shredded
- 5 oz fresh mushrooms, drained and sliced
- 1 cup milk
- 1 tablespoon Worcestershire sauce
- 1 can (6 oz) French fried onion rings, divided
- 1 teaspoon ground pepper
- Salt to taste

Directions

1. In the large bowl combine green beans, mushroom soup, cheddar cheese, fresh mushrooms, milk, sauce and pepper.
2. Stir in half of French fried onion rings.
3. Grace slow cooker lightly and put casserole mixture into the crockpot.
4. Cover and cook on low for 2 hours.
5. Sprinkle remaining onion rings on the top of the dish, cover and cook another 30-40 minutes.
6. Serve and enjoy.

Main Dishes

Potatoes with Bacon & Beans

Prep time: 15 minutes, cook time: 6 hours, servings: 8

Ingredients

- 7-8 bacon strips, chopped
- 1 pound fresh green beans, cut into 2-inch pieces
- ½ pound potatoes, peeled and cut into 1/2-inch cubes
- 1 medium onion, sliced
- ¼ cup chicken stock
- Salt and pepper, to taste

Directions

1. Cook chopped bacon in the skillet over medium heat, until crisp, for about 4-5 minutes.
2. Remove bacon to kitchen towels, dry and set aside until serving.
3. Mix chopped beans, potatoes, and onions in your crock pot. Pour in chicken stock and couple tablespoons grease from the skillet. Season with salt and pepper, to taste, cover and cook on low for 6 hours until potatoes are cooked and tender.
4. Add bacon, stir to combine and serve warm.

Pork Roast in Mustard Sauce

Prep time: 15 minutes, cook time: 4-4,5 hours, servings: 4-5

Ingredients

- 2-3 pound pork loin
- 2 tablespoons Italian seasoning
- 1 can (14 oz) cranberry sauce
- 3 tablespoons Dijon mustard
- 2 tablespoons olive oil
- Salt, to taste

Directions

1. Heat the olive oil in a large skillet. Brown pork roast from all sides for about 3-4 minutes.
2. Transfer meat to a slow cooker and season with salt and Italian seasoning. Pour in cranberry sauce and cover the cooker.
3. Cook on low for 4 hours until meat is tender. Remove pork roast to a plate.
4. Stir mustard into cooking juices.
5. Slice the pork loin and serve with cranberry-mustard sauce.

Sweet Potato Stew with Chicken

Prep time: 15 minutes, cook time: 4 hours, servings: 6-7

Ingredients

- 2 pounds chicken breasts, cubed
- 4 large sweet potatoes, peeled and cut into cubes
- 2 yellow potatoes, peeled and cubed
- 3 large carrots, sliced
- 2 cups chicken or vegetable stock
- 2 cans (15 fl oz each) tomatoes
- 2 teaspoons smoked paprika
- ½ teaspoon ground cumin
- 3 tablespoons fresh basil
- Salt and black pepper, to taste

Directions

1. Cut chicken breasts into 1-inch cubes and transfer to a slow cooker basket.
2. Do the same with potatoes. Add sliced carrots and tomatoes. Pour in stock and season with salt, pepper, and other spices. Stir to combine well.
3. Cover and cook on high for 4-5 hours or until meat become ready and tender.
4. Serve hot.

Outstanding Sweet Pork

Prep time: 10 minutes, cook time: 4 hours, servings: 5-6

Ingredients

- 2 pounds pork
- 2 cans Coke (not diet)
- 1 teaspoon garlic salt
- ½ cup brown sugar
- ¼ cup water
- 1 can (4 oz) green chilies, diced
- 1 can (10 oz) enchilada sauce

Directions

1. Take a large zip-lock bag and place the pork into it.
2. Add there 1 can of Coke, ½ cup of brown sugar. Make sure the pork dips into the marinade. Place the bag in the fridge for the whole night.
3. After that drain the marinade and put pork into the slow cooker.
4. Add ½ can of Coke, water and garlic salt over the meat.
5. Cook on high for at least 3-4 hours.
6. Once meat is almost ready shred it up with 2 forks.
7. Mix remaining Coke, green chilies, enchilada sauce and sugar in the large bowl.
8. Serve the pork with sauce and enjoy!

Creamy Potatoes with Bratwurst Sausage

Prep time: 15 minutes, cook time: 6 hours, servings: 6-8

Ingredients

- 2 pounds potatoes, peeled and cubed
- 2 pounds uncooked bratwurst sausage
- 2 cups half-and-half cream
- 1 large carrot, chopped
- 1 large onion, chopped
- 2 garlic cloves, crushed
- 1-2 celery ribs, chopped
- 1 green bell pepper, chopped
- 1/2 cup chicken stock
- 1 teaspoon dried basil
- 1 tablespoon cornstarch
- 3 tablespoons cold water
- Salt and black pepper to taste

Directions

1. Add potatoes, onions, carrot, celery, garlic and pepper to a slow cooker. Stir to combine. Top with bratwurst links.
2. Pour in chicken stock and season with salt, pepper and basil.
3. Cook on low for 6 hours until sausages are cooked.
4. Remove sausage and cut into 1-inch pieces. Add meat to the slow cooker and stir in half-and-half cream.
5. Combine cornstarch with water until smooth. Add to stew and stir well.

6. Cover and cook on high for addition 20-30 minutes until thickened and

Sweet Chicken Breast with Honey
Prep time: 10 minutes, cook time: 3 hours, servings: 3-4

Ingredients

- 1 pound chicken breast, skinless
- ¼ teaspoon ground pepper
- ½ cup honey
- ¼ cup soy sauce
- ½ teaspoon salt
- 1 onion, chopped
- 1/8 cup ketchup
- 1 tablespoon vegetable oil
- 1 clove garlic, minced
- ¼ teaspoon red pepper flakes

Directions

1. Season chicken breasts in both sides with salt and pepper. Put into the slow cooker.
2. In the medium bowl mix soy sauce, honey, chopped onion, ketchup, garlic, and pepper flakes. Pour over chicken with mixture.
3. Cook on low for at least 3 hours.
4. Cut cooked chicken into bite size pieces, return to the crockpot and cover with sauce.
5. Serve with rice or noodles.

Slow Cooker Chicken Adobo

Prep time: 15 minutes, cook time: 6-7 hours, servings: 5-6

Ingredients

- 3 pounds chicken thighs, bone-in
- 4 garlic cloves
- 2 medium-sized onions, sliced
- 5 tablespoons soy sauce
- 4 tablespoons apple vinegar
- 1 tablespoon garlic powder
- 1-inch piece fresh ginger, sliced
- Salt and ground black pepper, to taste
- 2 tablespoons olive oil

Directions

1. Season chicken thighs with salt, pepper, and garlic powder from all sides.
2. Preheat olive oil in the large skillet. Brown chicken on both sides until skin is golden for about 5-7 minutes.
3. Add 1 tablespoon of olive oil in the slow cooker and place onion slices on the bottom.
4. Place browned chicken thighs on the top of the onions. Lay garlic cloves and sliced ginger.
5. Pour soy sauce and vinegar over chicken and season with salt and black pepper, to taste.
6. Cover and cook on low for about 7-8 hours, until chicken tender and cooked.

Famous Santa Fe Chicken

Prep time: 13 minutes, cook time: 8-10 hours, servings: 4-6

Ingredients

- 1 ½ pounds chicken breast, skinless
- 1 can (14 oz) tomatoes with green chilies, diced
- 1 can (14 oz) black beans
- 6-8 oz frozen corn
- ½ cup fresh cilantro, chopped
- 1 can (14 oz) chicken broth
- 2 shallot, chopped
- 1 teaspoon garlic powder
- 1 teaspoon onion powder
- 1 teaspoon cumin
- 1 teaspoon cayenne pepper
- Salt and pepper for seasoning

Directions

1. In the large bowl add chicken broth, beans, corn, tomatoes, cilantro, shallot, garlic and onion powders, cumin, cayenne pepper, salt, and stir to combine.
2. Place this mixture in the slow cooker.
3. Season chicken breasts and lay them on the top of other ingredients inside the crockpot.
4. Cook on low for 8-10 hours.
5. In an hour before serving remove chicken from the slow cooker and shred.
6. Return chicken into the slow cooker and stir with other ingredients.

7. Serve and season with salt and pepper to taste.

Amazing Tender Chicken with Mushrooms

Prep time: 10 minutes, cook time: 6 hours, servings: 4-5

Ingredients

- 1 ½ pounds chicken breasts, skinless and trimmed of fat
- 2 cups chicken broth
- 1 middle onion, minced
- 6 cloves garlic, minced
- 1 tablespoon olive oil
- 1 tablespoon tomato paste
- 1 teaspoon dried thyme, crushed
- 1 lb fresh mushrooms, sliced
- 2 tablespoons white wine vinegar
- 2 tablespoons quick-cooking tapioca
- ½ cup Parmesan cheese
- 1 tablespoon dried parsley
- Salt and pepper for seasoning

Directions

1. In microwave-safe bowl mix onion, garlic, olive oil, tomato paste, thyme. Cook for about 5 minutes until onion becomes tender. Pour into a slow cooker.
2. Season chicken with salt and pepper.
3. In a bowl stir the chicken breasts, mushrooms, broth, vinegar and tapioca and put the mixture in the slow cooker.
4. Cover and cook on low for 4-6 hours.

5. Remove the chicken and shred it into large pieces using two forks.
6. Remove extra fat from the surface and place the chicken back into the slow cooker.
7. Add cheese and dried parsley.
8. Season to taste and serve with pasta or rice.

Spicy Pork Chili

Prep time: 10 minutes, cook time: 6 hours, servings: 6-8

Ingredients

- 2 pounds boneless pork, cut into 1/2-inch cubes
- 2 medium onions, chopped
- 3 garlic cloves, minced
- 1 can (15 oz) black beans, rinsed and drained
- 1 can (28 oz) crushed tomatoes
- 1 can (4 oz) chopped green chilies
- 2 cups corn, frozen
- 1 cup beef or chicken stock
- 1 tablespoon chili powder
- Salt and black pepper, to taste
- ¼ cup freshly chopped cilantro
- 1 tablespoon olive oil

Directions

1. Heat the olive oil in a skillet and cook pork over medium-high heat for 3-4 minutes from all sides until browned.
2. Transfer pork chunks with cooking juices to a slow cooker. Add tomatoes, onions, garlic, corn, stock, chilies and all seasoning.
3. Covet the lid and cook on low for 6 hours until meat is cooked and tender.
4. Sprinkle with freshly chopped cilantro and serve.

Adorable Crockpot Italian Chicken
Prep time: 10 minutes, cook time: 5 hours, servings: 4

Ingredients

- 2-4 chicken breasts, boneless and skinless
- 1 package (8 oz) cream cheese, softened
- 1 can cream of chicken soup
- 1 package Italian dressing seasoning
- Pasta or rice to serve

Directions

1. Prepare chicken and transfer in the slow cooker.
2. Combine softened cream cheese, cream of chicken and Italian seasoning and place evenly over the chicken.
3. Cover and cook on high up to 5 hours or until chicken will be prepared and fully tender.
4. Serve over cooked pasta or rice.

Jerky Chicken

Prep time: 10 minutes, cook time: 4 hours, servings: 6

Ingredients

- 6 large chicken legs
- 1 medium carrot, chopped
- 1 small onion, chopped
- 3 garlic cloves, crushed
- 2 teaspoons crushed red pepper
- 2 teaspoons garlic powder
- 2 teaspoons onion powder
- 2 teaspoons smoked paprika
- 2 teaspoons dried rosemary
- 1 teaspoon dried thyme
- 1 teaspoon ground ginger
- Salt and black pepper, to taste
- 1 teaspoon liquid smoke
- 3 tablespoons brown sugar
- 1 container of Caribbean jerk marinade
- 2 cups water

Directions

1. Place chicken legs in your slow cooker basket. Add all dried seasonings and ingredients.
2. Add carrots, onions, and garlic. Pour in marinade, liquid smoke and water to cover all the chicken.
3. Stir to combine well.
4. Cover and cook on high for 4 hours.
5. Serve and enjoy.

Potato Stew with Vegetables and Spices
Prep time: 8 minutes, cook time: 5 hours, servings: 6-8

Ingredients

- 3 pounds potatoes, diced
- 1 medium onion, minced
- 4 medium tomatoes
- 2 teaspoon mustard seeds
- 1 teaspoon ground ginger
- 1 teaspoon garam masala
- 1 teaspoon turmeric
- ½ teaspoon ground cumin
- ½ teaspoon chili powder
- ¼ cup dried chili flakes
- 3 tablespoon Olive oil
- Salt and ground black pepper to taste

Directions

1. In a bowl mix spices expect of mustard seeds: ginger, garam masala, turmeric, cumin, chili powder.
2. Prepare vegetables, wash, peel and cube potatoes, mince onion.
3. Wash tomatoes, squeeze out seeds and chop them into little pieces.
4. Hit some olive oil, add mustard seeds and cook until popping.
5. Add onion; cook for near 5 minutes until transparent.
6. Add spices and cook for 3-4 minutes to get the flavor going.

7. Add cubed potatoes. Stir and make sure that every cube gets into spice mixture.
8. Add diced tomatoes.
9. Salt and add some ground pepper to taste.
10. Cook on low for 5 hours or until ready.

Buffalo Chicken Pasta

Prep time: 10 minutes, cook time: 4 hours, servings: 8-10

Ingredients

- 2 ½ pounds chicken breasts, boneless and skinless
- 1 large onion, chopped
- 3 garlic cloves, minced
- 1 pack (16 oz) penne pasta or spaghetti
- 2 cans (10 oz each) condensed cream of chicken soup
- 6 tablespoons Buffalo sauce
- 2 cups shredded Mozzarella cheese
- 1 ½ cups low-fat sour cream
- 5 tablespoons ranch dressing
- Salt and black pepper, to taste

Directions

1. Cut the chicken tenders into 1-inch cubes and place to a slow cooker. Add onions, garlic, condensed cream, sauce, salt and pepper. Stir to combine.
2. Cover and cook for 4 hours.
3. Meanwhile, cook pasta according to package directions for almost cooked. Drain.
4. When chicken cooked, add cheese and stir until melted. Add pasta, sour cream and ranch dressing.

Pork Chops with Tomatoes

Prep time: 15 minutes, cook time: 8 hours, servings: 6-8

Ingredients

- 6-8 pork chops, bone-in
- 1 large onion, chopped
- 2 medium carrots, chopped
- 1 can (15 oz) diced tomatoes
- 1 teaspoon dried oregano
- 2 teaspoon dried dill
- 3 tablespoons balsamic vinegar
- 1 tablespoon olive oil
- 1 teaspoon salt
- ¼ teaspoon black pepper

Directions

1. Heat the olive oil in a large skillet. Brown pork chops in batches for 4-5 minutes until brown and then transfer to a slow cooker.
2. In the same skillet sauté onions and carrots for 3-4 minutes and also transfer to a slow cooker.
3. Add dry herbs, stir in tomatoes and vinegar. Cover and cook on low for 8 hours.
4. Serve.

Herbs & Wine Veal

Prep time: 10 minutes, cook time: 6-7 hours, servings: 4-5

Ingredients

- 2 pounds veal cut
- 4-5 garlic cloves
- 1 teaspoon dried thyme
- 1 teaspoon dried rosemary
- 1 teaspoon dried sage
- ½ cup butter
- 1 bottle dry red wine
- Salt and black pepper, to taste

Directions

1. Mix all dry ingredients and herbs in a bowl. Rub the meat with herbs and transfer to a slow cooker basket.
2. Pour in wine to cover the meat. If it's not enough you may pour in some water.
3. Lay butter on top of the meat.
4. Cover and cook on low for 6-7 hours until meat tender.
5. Serve with mashed potatoes, noodles or rice.

Pork Chops Barbecue with Apples and Onions

Prep time: 5 minutes, cook time: 4 hours, servings: 5

Ingredients

- 4 large apples, cored and sliced
- 2 large onions, sliced
- 8 large pork chops
- ½ cup water
- 1 jar (8 oz) barbecue sauce
- 1 teaspoon salt
- 1/4 teaspoon black pepper

Directions

1. Cover pork chops with salt and pepper and transfer to a slow cooker.
2. Slice apples and onions and cover the meat. Pour in water, close the lid and cook on high for 3 hours.
3. Meanwhile, combine barbecue sauce with water.
4. When meat is almost ready, open the lid and stir in sauce to a slow cooker. Cook for 30-40 minutes more.
5. Serve hot and enjoy.

Black Beans and Beef Stew

Prep time: 5 minutes, cook time: 8 hours, servings: 4

Ingredients

- 1 pound beef
- 1 large onion, chopped
- 1 large potato, diced
- 1 large carrot, chopped
- 2 cans (15 oz each) black beans, rinsed and drained
- 4 cups chicken broth
- 1 teaspoon chili powder
- 1 teaspoon ground cumin
- ½ teaspoon salt
- ¼ teaspoon ground black pepper
- 1 tablespoon olive oil

Directions

1. Cut beef into 1-inch pieces and transfer to a slow cooker pot. Add all another ingredients, and season with salt, pepper, cumin, and chili powder. Pour in broth and stir to combine well.
2. Close the lid and cook for 7-8 hours on low.
3. Serve with freshly chopped herbs on your preference.

Asian Pork Chops

Prep time: 20 minutes, cook time: 6 hours, servings: 4

Ingredients

- 8 pork chops, boneless
- 3 tablespoons sugar
- 4 garlic cloves, chopped
- 1 teaspoon grated ginger
- ½ cup soy sauce
- ½ cup ketchup
- Salt and ground black pepper, to taste

Directions

1. In a large mixing bowl combine pork chops, sugar, grated ginger, soy sauce, ketchup, and season with salt and pepper.
2. Transfer marinated pork chops to a slow cooker pot and cook on high for 6 hours.
3. Serve with steamed vegetables or egg noodles.

Clean Eating Crock Pot Chuck Roast

Prep time: 45 minutes, cook time: 5 hours, servings: 8

Ingredients

- 3 pounds chuck roast
- 4 large potatoes
- 1 large carrot, chopped
- 2 medium onions, diced
- 3 garlic cloves, minced
- 2 cups water
- 1 cup chicken or beef stock
- 1 teaspoon Italian seasoning
- 1 teaspoon salt
- ¼ teaspoon black pepper, ground

Directions

1. Cut vegetables and transfer to a slow cooker.
2. Rub chuck roast with salt, pepper, and Italian seasoning and place over diced vegetables. Pour in stock and water. Make sure that liquid is covering all ingredients.
3. Close the lid and cook on high for 5 hours.
4. Serve with juices and enjoy.

Slow Cooker Beef Brisket

Prep time: 20 minutes, cook time: 6 hours, servings: 8

Ingredients

- 2 pounds beef brisket without fat
- 4 tablespoons ketchup
- 1 cup water
- 1 large onion, chopped
- 2 tablespoons vinegar
- 1 tablespoon mustard
- 1 tablespoon sugar
- ½ teaspoon salt
- ¼ teaspoon black pepper

Directions

1. Cover beef brisket with salt and pepper and transfer to a slow cooker. Add chopped onion and pour in water.
2. Close the lid and cook on low for 6 hours.
3. Meanwhile, combine ketchup, vinegar, mustard and couple tablespoons of water in the mixing bowl. Sauté the mixture in a heatproof pan over low heat for 10-15 minutes.
4. When meat becomes ready, slice it and cover with sauce. Enjoy.

Smoked Up Baby Potatoes with Beef

Prep time: 10 minutes, cook time: 5 hours, servings: 6

Ingredients

- 2 pounds beef
- 2 pounds baby potatoes
- 2 large tomatoes, chopped
- 3 garlic cloves, minced
- 1 medium-sized onion, chopped
- 1 tablespoon smoked paprika
- ½ teaspoon chili powder
- 3 tablespoons ketchup
- 1 teaspoon cumin
- 5 tablespoons barbecue sauce
- ¼ cup salsa
- 1 cup frozen corn
- 1 tablespoon olive oil
- Salt and pepper, to taste

Directions

1. Cut beef into 1-inch cubes and transfer to a slow cooker. Add 1 tablespoon of olive oil and brown meat using Sauté mode.
2. Add baby potatoes, onions, tomatoes, and garlic, chili powder, cumin, salsa and barbecue sauces. Mix well and cook on high for 4-5 hours until meat is almost done.
3. Add frozen corn, season with salt and pepper and cook for 1 hour more.

4. Serve and enjoy.

Beer Chili Beans with Bratwurst Sausage

Prep time: 10 minutes, cook time: 5 hours, servings: 6-8

Ingredients

- 1 pound fully cooked beer bratwurst links, sliced
- 1 large onion, chopped
- 2 garlic cloves, crushed
- 2 tablespoons chili seasoning
- 1 can (15 oz) Southwestern black beans, undrained
- 1 can (15 oz) pinto beans, rinsed and drained
- 1 can (15 oz) white kidney or cannellini beans, rinsed and drained
- 1 can (10 oz) diced tomatoes and green chilies, undrained
- 1 can (14 oz) Italian diced tomatoes, undrained
- ½ teaspoon salt
- Chopped fresh parsley, optional

Directions

1. Cut beer bratwurst sausage into 1-inch slices and place to a slow cooker. Add onions and garlic, and pour in beans and tomatoes. Season with salt and chili mix. Stir to combine.
2. Cover and cook on low for 4,5-5 hours. When ready sprinkle with freshly chopped parsley and serve warm.

Tender Beef Stroganoff

Prep time: 6 minutes, cook time: 5-6 hours, servings: 4-5

Ingredients

- 2 pounds stew beef
- ½ cup beef broth
- 16 oz fresh mushrooms, sliced
- 2 packages onion soup mix
- 3 tablespoon Worcestershire sauce
- 2 ½ cup sour cream
- 4 oz cream cheese, softened
- 1 package cooked egg noodles for serving

Directions

1. Put stew meat, broth, sliced mushrooms, soup mix, Worcestershire sauce into the slow cooker and cook on low for 4-6 hours until meat prepared.'
2. After that add sour cream and cream cheese into the cooker, stir the mixture until combined and smooth.
3. Serve over cooked egg noodles.
4. Enjoy.

Sweet Potatoes with Coconut and Pecans

Prep time: 10 minutes, cook time: 4 hours, servings: 8

Ingredients

- 3 pounds sweet potatoes, cubed into 1-inch pieces
- ½ cup pecans, chopped
- ½ cup coconut flakes
- 4 tablespoons sugar
- ½ teaspoon ground cinnamon
- ½ teaspoon coconut extract
- ½ teaspoon vanilla extract
- 2 tablespoons butter, melted
- A pinch of salt

Directions

1. Mix chopped pecans, coconut flakes, sugar, cinnamon and salt in a bowl. Add melted butter and stir to combine.
2. Place sweet potatoes to a slow cooker and cover with pecan mixture.
3. Cook on low for 4 hours until potatoes become tender and cooked.
4. Add coconut and vanilla extracts, stir to combine and serve.

Easy Beef Steak

Prep time: 10 minutes, cook time: 6 hours, servings: 4-5

Ingredients

- 2 pounds beef round steak
- 1 large onion, sliced
- 1 garlic clove, minced
- 2 tablespoons all-purpose flour
- ½ cup tomato paste
- ½ teaspoon salt
- ¼ teaspoon ground black pepper

Directions

1. Divide steak into 4 pieces. Cover each piece with flour, salt and pepper.
2. Slice onion and transfer to a slow cooker.
3. Lay the meat over onions and cover with tomato paste. Cover and cook on low for 5-6 hours until meat is tender.
4. Serve with cooked rice or potatoes.

Side Dishes

Jamaican Curry Chicken

Prep time: 15 minutes, cook time: 2 hours, servings: 5-6

Ingredients

- 2 pounds chicken breasts, skinless and boneless
- 2 medium-sized onions, chopped
- 2 large potatoes, peeled and diced
- 2 garlic cloves
- ½ bell pepper, diced
- 2 tablespoons Jamaican spices
- 3 tablespoons Curry powder
- ½ tablespoon dried thyme
- 1 cup water
- ¼ teaspoon black pepper
- 1 teaspoon salt

Directions

1. Wash chicken, dry with kitchen towels, and cut into 2-inch pieces. Transfer to a large bowl.
2. Add diced potatoes, onions, garlic, bell peppers and all seasoning. Stir to combine well and set aside at least for 30 minutes.
3. Place chicken & vegetable mixture to a slow cooker and pour in water.
4. Cover and cook on high for 2 hours.
5. Serve hot. Sprinkle with freshly chopped herbs if desired.

Delicious Chicken with Mushrooms
Prep time: 17 minutes, cook time: 3-4 hours, servings: 5-7

Ingredients

- 2 ½ pounds chicken breast, without bones and skin
- 1 medium onion, chopped
- 2-3 garlic cloves, minced
- 3 cups fresh mushrooms on your preference, sliced
- 1 cup chicken or vegetable stock
- 3 tablespoons tomato paste
- 1/2 cup dry red wine
- 1 tablespoon dried basil
- 1 tablespoon dried oregano
- 1 teaspoon salt
- ¼ teaspoon black pepper
- ¼ cup Parmesan cheese, grated

Directions

1. Lay sliced mushrooms, onions, and garlic on the bottom of your slow cooker.
2. Cut chicken into 2-inch pieces and place on top of the vegetables.
3. In a separate bowl combine stock, tomato paste, wine, basil, oregano, salt, and pepper. Mix well.
4. Pour the mixture over chicken and vegetables.
5. Cover and cook on high for 3-4 hours, until chicken is tender.
6. Serve with noodles or mashed potatoes and top with grated Parmesan cheese.

Beef and Broccoli Penne

Prep time: 10 minutes, cook time: 2-3 hours, servings: 5

Ingredients

- 1 pound ground beef
- 1 broccoli head (nearly 1 pound) cut into florets
- 1 large onion, sliced
- 2 garlic cloves, minced
- 1 teaspoon dried oregano
- 1 teaspoon dried basil
- 1 teaspoon dried thyme
- 1 can (14 oz) diced tomatoes with juices
- 2 cups beef or chicken stock
- 2 tablespoons tomato paste
- 2 cups Penne, cooked
- ½ cup shredded Cheddar cheese
- 1 tablespoon olive oil
- Salt and pepper, to taste

Directions

1. Heat the olive oil in a large skillet over medium heat and cook ground beef with garlic until no longer pink, breaking meat apart with wooden spoon.
2. Transfer browned meat to a slow cooker.
3. Add broccoli florets, onions, tomatoes with juices, and tomato paste to a slow cooker. Season with salt and pepper, add dried herbs and pour in stock.
4. Cover and cook on high for 2-3 hours.
5. Serve with cooker Penne pasta and top with shredded cheese.

Salsa Chicken in Sour Cream

Prep time: 10 minutes, cook time: 3 hours, servings: 5

Ingredients

- 3 pounds chicken breasts, boneless and skinless, cut in halves
- 6-8 slices cooked ham
- 3 tablespoons taco seasoning
- 2 cups salsa
- 1/2 cup low-fat sour cream

Directions

1. Cut chicken in halves and cover each piece with ham. Roll up and secure with toothpicks. Rub with taco seasoning.
2. Transfer chicken pieces to a slow cooker and pour over with salsa and sour cream.
3. Cover the lid and cook on high for 3 hours, until chicken becomes ready.
4. Serve with mashed potatoes or steamed rice.

Creole Chicken Stew

Prep time: 10 minutes, cook time: 4 hours, servings: 5-6

Ingredients

- 2 pounds chicken breasts
- 2 medium onions, sliced
- 4 stalks celery, chopped
- 3 large tomatoes, chopped
- 1 large green bell pepper, chopped
- 4 garlic cloves, minced
- 3 tablespoons tomato paste
- 1 cup chicken stock
- ¼ teaspoon black pepper
- ½ teaspoon salt
- 1 tablespoon Cajun seasoning
- 1 teaspoon dried thyme
- 2 tablespoons olive oil
- Freshly chopped parsley for garnish

Directions

1. Sprinkle slow cooker pot with the olive oil and set the cooker on Sauté mode. Add sliced onions and minced garlic and sauté for 5-7 minutes, until tender. Add celery and bell pepper, stir to combine and cook for another 3-5 minutes.
2. Add diced tomatoes, tomato paste and pour in stock. Mix well and sauté for 2-3 minutes more.
3. Cut chicken breasts into 2-inch pieces and transfer to a slow cooker. Season with salt, pepper, thyme and

Cajun mixture. Close the lid and cook on high for 3 hours.
4. Garnish with freshly chopped parsley, serve and enjoy.

Creamy Chicken with Noodles
Prep time: 7 minutes, cook time: 2 hours, servings: 5-6

Ingredients

- 2 pounds cooked chicken breasts, cut into large chunks
- 1 medium onion, chopped
- 1 little carrot, diced
- 12 oz condensed cream of chicken soup
- 6 tablespoons mayonnaise
- 2 tablespoons all-purpose flour
- 1 cup frozen broccoli florets, defrosted
- 1 teaspoon curry powder
- Salt and black pepper, to taste
- 2 cups cooked egg noodles

Directions

1. In a large bowl combine cooked chicken breasts, chopped onions, carrots, condensed cream, mayonnaise, flour, defrosted broccoli florets. Add curry powder, salt and pepper, to taste. Mix well.
2. Transfer the mixture to a slow cooker basket, cover the lid and cook on high for 2 hours.
3. When ready, serve the chicken with egg noodles.
4. You can also sprinkle with grated cheese to your taste.

Chicken Paprikash Noodles
Prep time: 8 minutes, cook time: 5 hours, servings: 8

Ingredients

- 2 pounds chicken breasts, boneless and skinless
- 2 medium onions, diced
- 3 garlic cloves, minced
- 2 cups egg noodles, cooked
- Couple bay leaves
- ¼ teaspoon ground black pepper
- 1 teaspoon paprika
- ½ cup chicken stock
- 1 cup cream cheese
- 1 teaspoon salt
- 2 tablespoons olive oil

Directions

1. Sprinkle slow cooker pot with olive oil and sauté garlic and onion for about 5-7 minutes, stirring occasionally.
2. Cut chicken breasts and place to a slow cooker. Sauté for 5 minutes more. Add bay leaves, black pepper, salt, paprika. Pour in chicken stock and mix well. Cover the lid and cook for 5 hours, until cooked.
3. Serve with cooked egg noodles and stir in cream cheese. Enjoy.

Soup Recipes

Easy Potato Soup

Prep time: 25 minutes, cook time: 5 hours, servings: 5-6

Ingredients

- 2 pounds potatoes, cubed and divided
- 2 cups water
- 3 tablespoon butter
- 2/3 cup sour cream
- 1/2 cup Cheddar cheese, shredded
- 1/2 pound cooked ham, cubed
- 2 celery ribs, chopped
- 1 medium onion, chopped
- 2 garlic cloves, minced
- 1 teaspoon paprika
- Salt and black pepper, to taste

Directions

1. Add 1 ½ pound of cubed potatoes in a saucepan and bring to a boil over high heat. Reduce heat and cook for 12 minutes or until cooked.
2. Remove from the heat and mash potatoes with potato masher. Stir in butter.
3. In a slow cooker add cooked ham, chopped celery, onions, and garlic. Season with salt, pepper and paprika, and stir it remaining potatoes. Also add mashed potatoes and shredded cheese. Stir to combine.

4. Cover with lid and cook on low for 4,5-5 hours, until potatoes are tender. Add sour cream and serve.

Spicy Bean Soup with Turkey

Prep time: 7 minutes, cook time: 4 ½ hours, servings: 5-6

Ingredients

- 1 pound turkey breast, cooked and cubed
- 2 cans (15 oz each) beans, rinsed
- 3 cups chicken stock
- 1 can (10 oz) diced tomatoes with green chilies
- 1 cup salsa
- ½ teaspoon dried basil
- ½ teaspoon smoked paprika
- ¼ teaspoon cayenne pepper
- ¼ teaspoon curry
- A pinch of salt

Directions

1. Cut cooked turkey into 1-inch cubes and place to a slow cooker. Add beans and diced tomatoes, stir in salsa and pour in chicken stock.
2. Add herbs and spices and stir to combine.
3. Cover and cook on low for 5 hours.
4. Serve hot.

Kale Soup with Italian Sausage

Prep time: 15 minutes, cook time: 6 hours, servings: 7-8

Ingredients

- 6 cups chopped fresh kale
- 1 pound Italian sausage (you may use any on your preference)
- 3 large carrots, chopped
- 1 large onion, chopped
- 4 garlic cloves, minced
- 2 cans (15 oz) kidney beans, rinsed and drained
- 1 can (28 oz) crushed tomatoes
- 1 teaspoon dried basil
- 1 tablespoon olive oil
- Salt and black pepper to taste
- ¼ cup grated Parmesan for serving

Directions

1. Heat the olive oil in a large skillet over high heat and cook sausage for 5-7 minutes until no longer pink, breaking into small pieces.
2. Place browned sausage in a slow cooker pot. Add kale, carrots, onions and garlic. Stir in beans and tomatoes and mix well.
3. Cover lid and cook on low for 6 hours until sausage and veggies are tender.

Serve warm and top with grated Parmesan.

Chicken Tomato Soup

Prep time: 10 minutes, cook time: 4 ½ hours, servings: 7-8

Ingredients

- 1 pound chicken breasts
- 1 large onion, chopped
- 2 large potatoes, peeled and cubed
- 1 small carrot, chopped
- 2-3 garlic cloves, crushed
- 2 cups frozen corn
- 1 can (10 oz) tomato puree
- 4 cups chicken stock
- 1 can (10 oz) diced tomatoes
- 1 teaspoon ground cumin
- 1 teaspoon chili powder
- 1/8 teaspoon cayenne pepper
- ½ to 1 teaspoon salt
- ½ cup fresh chopped parsley

Directions

1. Cut chicken into 1-inch cubes. Also peel and cut potatoes into 1-inch cubes. Add all ingredients to a slow cooker and season with herbs and spices.
2. Pour in chicken stock, cover and cook on low for 4-5 hours.
3. Sprinkle with freshly chopped parsley and serve hot.

Delicious Vegetable Soup with Beef Chunks

Prep time: 10 minutes, cook time: 6 hours, servings: 8

Ingredients

- 1 pound beef steak, cut into 1/2-inch pieces
- 1 cup frozen mixed vegetables
- 2 large potatoes, cubed
- 1 large onion, diced
- 3 celery ribs, sliced
- 2 medium carrots, sliced
- 1 can (14 oz) diced tomatoes with juices
- 4 cups beef or chicken stock
- 2 tablespoons Italian seasoning
- Salt and pepper, to taste

Directions

1. Cut the meat and sauté in a skillet over medium-high heat for 5-7 minutes until lightly brown. Transfer to a slow cooker.
2. Add prepared veggies, sprinkle with seasoning, salt and pepper, and pour in stock.
3. Cover and cook on high for nearly 6 hours until meat and vegetables are cooked and tender.
4. Ladle into serving plates, sprinkle with freshly chopped herbs and serve.

Meaty Barley Lentil Soup

Prep time: 7 minutes, cook time: 7 hours, servings: 8-10

Ingredients

- 1 pound ground beef
- 2 cans (15 oz each) tomatoes, roughly chopped
- 4 large potatoes, cut into 1-inch pieces
- 1 large onion chopped
- 1 medium-sized carrot, chopped
- 1 cup dried lentils
- ½ cup dried barley
- 3 beef bouillon cubes
- 7-8 cups water
- 2 tablespoons olive oil
- Salt and black pepper, to taste

Directions

1. Heat the olive oil in a large skillet over high heat. Cook onions for 3-5 minutes until translucent. Add ground beef and cook for 3-4 minutes more until no longer pink. Transfer the mixture to a slow cooker.
2. Add vegetables, lentils, and barley.
3. Whisk water, beef bouillon cubes, salt, and pepper in a separate bowl. Pour over meat. Cover and cook on low for 7 hours until barley and lentils are cooked.

Snacks and Desserts

Caramelized Onions

Prep time: 6 minutes, cook time: 2 hours, servings: 6

Ingredients

- 4 large onions, sliced
- 4 tablespoons melted butter
- 1 tablespoon sugar
- ½ teaspoon salt
- ¼ teaspoon black pepper

Directions

1. Melt the butter in the slow cooker using Sauté mode.
2. Slice onions and transfer to a slow cooker pot.
3. Season with salt and black pepper and stir to combine.
4. Cook on high for 2 hours.
5. Serve with any meal like side dish or topping for pizza or burgers.

Slow Cooker Apples

Prep time: 10 minutes, cook time: 3 hours, servings: 6

Ingredients

- 6 large apples (choose medium sized)
- 4 cups granola
- 4 tablespoons melted butter
- 2 tablespoons maple syrup
- Ice cream or whipped cream for garnish

Directions

1. Cut off the top of each apple. Core apples, remove and discard seeds.
2. Fill each apple with granola and drizzle with melted butter. Pour a teaspoon of maple syrup in the apple and place them to a slow cooker.
3. Cook with closed lid on low for 2-3 hours.
4. Serve with ice cream or whipped cream and enjoy.

Crock Pot Stewed Plums

Prep time: 15 minutes, cook time: 2 hours, servings: 6

Ingredients

- 15 large sweet plums
- 1 cup brown sugar
- 1 teaspoon ground cinnamon
- 6 tablespoons water
- 2 tablespoons cornstarch

Directions

1. Combine cold water and cornstarch in a small mixing bowl. Stir well and set aside.
2. Wash and dry plums. Cut them, remove and discard seeds.
3. Place plums into a slow cooker and sprinkle with brown sugar and cinnamon.
4. Pour in cornstarch mixture and mix well.
5. Close the lid and cook on low for 2 hours.
6. When ready, serve stewed plums with yogurt or ice cream.
7. Enjoy!

Peanuts with Chocolate

Prep time: 5 minutes, cook time: 2 hours, servings: 8

Ingredients

- 2 cups dry roasted unsalted peanuts
- ½ cup semi-sweet chocolate chips
- 1 dark chocolate bar of your choice
- 1 white chocolate bar of your choice

Directions

1. Place peanuts and choco chips to a slow cooker. Crush chocolate bars in a mixing bowl and transfer to a slow cooker too. Mix and close the lid.
2. Cook on low for 2 hours.
3. Let peanuts chill lightly, then cut and serve. Enjoy

Conclusion

Thank you again for downloading my cookbook! I Hope this book helps you to know more interesting and tasty recipes or inspire you to create your own unique dishes.

Note from the author:

If you've enjoyed this book, I'd greatly appreciate if you could leave an honest review on Amazon. Reviews are very important to us authors, and it only takes a minute for to post.

Thank you!

Manufactured by Amazon.ca
Acheson, AB

11876039R00044